KINGFISHER

First published 2012 by Kingfisher
an imprint of Macmillan Children's Books
a division of Macmillan Publishers Limited
20 New Wharf Road, London N1 9RR
Basingstoke and Oxford
Associated companies throughout the world
www.panmacmillan.com

Illustrations by: Peter Bull Art Studio
Designer: Samantha Richiardi

Special thanks to Ray Bryant and Peter Winfield

ISBN 978-0-7534-3424-6

1 3 5 7 9 8 6 4 2
1TR/0712/WKT/UG/140WFO

A CIP catalogue record for this book is available from the British Library.

Printed in China

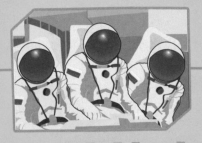

WARNING NOTES

The escape techniques described in this book are great fun to learn, and could be useful to you sometime in the future. However, many of them should be employed only when it is appropriate to do so, for example when your life is in peril and there are no safer options. Use your common sense.

Make sure that you have back-up when you go on an expedition or expose yourself to a risky situation, and never take part in any of the activities featured on the following pages by yourself. Always follow safety advice from professionally trained experts or responsible adults. This book is not intended to be a substitute for either.

Obey all laws and regulations, including those that control the use of fire and signalling equipment. Respect the rights of other individuals, and also animals and plants.

To the fullest extent permitted by applicable law, the publisher and author of *Escape* do not accept liability for injuries or loss of any kind that may occur as a result of the proper or improper use of the information in this book.

CONTENTS

ACCIDENTS AND EMERGENCIES

Accidents and emergencies happen suddenly with very little warning. It is natural to feel shocked and panicked if you are involved in one, but you must pull yourself together quickly. By staying calm, you will be better able to make smart decisions that could save your life. Of course, to make these decisions, you need to know in advance what they should be. In some cases, you can be extra prepared by having a survival kit at the ready.

Aeroplane crashes are very rare and nearly all of them have survivors. If you ever find yourself aboard a plane that needs to crash land, put these steps into action.

CRASH COURSE

STEP 1 Fasten your seat belt and adopt a brace position to stop yourself flying forwards on impact. Either hold your head with your hands on the seat in front of you, or bend your body forwards and hug your legs.

STEP 2 Once the plane has stopped, get out without delay. Follow the floor lights to your nearest exit. If the cabin fills with smoke, stoop and walk. This posture will help you to avoid the suffocating cloud of fumes.

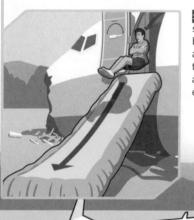

STEP 3 Jump onto the inflatable slide at the exit. To avoid friction burns, keep your heels up and your arms crossed over your chest on the way down. At the bottom, move away from the slide and wait for the emergency services.

The helicopter's engine has failed and the aircraft is dropping like a stone. But you're in luck! There is water below and it will cushion the impact. Your craft will sink – however, you can escape from it.

⊕ DOWN AND OUT

STEP 1 Put on your life jacket, but don't inflate it. Fasten your harness over it. Most of the helicopter's weight is on the top of the craft, so get ready for it to roll as it sinks. Your harness will stop you from being flung about when this happens.

STEP 2 Wait for the motion to stop, then feel about the cabin to find reference points that you recognize. Use these points to locate the door handle. As soon as you find it, open the door, release your harness and push yourself out.

STEP 3 Don't kick too hard when you leave the craft, as you could injure passengers behind you. Once you are clear of the helicopter, inflate your life jacket. This will help you to rise. Hold your hands above your head to protect it from debris.

→ PREPARE FOR SPLASHDOWN

● Familiarize yourself with, and map out in your head, the series of reference points that you would use to feel your way to the door handle. Reference points could include your seat, an arm rest and a window.

SOS ISS!

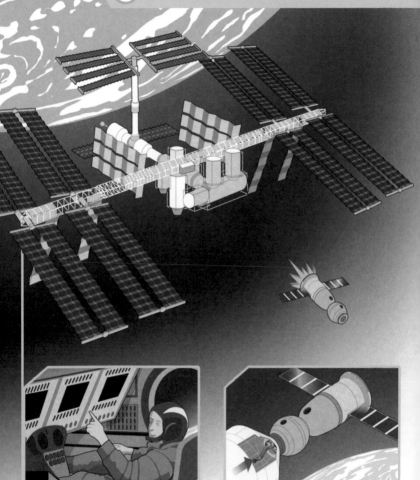

STEP 1 Try to remember the evacuation procedure: shut down some of the ISS systems, and close hatches and window shutters. Be quick, but stay calm.

STEP 2 Head to the Zvezda Service Module and find the docking port. Here you will find a Soyuz spacecraft already prepared with air pressure equalized inside.

Every ship needs a lifeboat, even a spaceship. The International Space Station is no exception. At 350km above Earth, it's far away from home, but the Soyuz evacuation craft is on hand in case of emergencies.

STEP 3 Climb into the Descent Module. Soyuz has three modules, and this is the only one that will survive the trip back to Earth. The other two modules are discarded before re-entry – they burn up in the atmosphere.

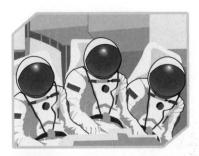

STEP 4 There is room for two other crew members. Help them into their custom-made, cushioned seats – and close the ISS hatch behind you.

STEP 5 Strap in tightly: the Soyuz takes two days to reach and dock with the ISS, but the return trip is a very swift 3.5 hours.

STEP 6 Use the eight hydrogen-peroxide thrusters to control your angle and height. Deploy the parachute to slow down once you are inside Earth's atmosphere.

STEP 7 Get out your phrasebook: you will touch down on the vast plains of Kazakhstan in central Asia. A team has been sent to pick you up.

TOP FIVE REASONS TO EVACUATE THE ISS

- Collision with space debris, such as old bits of satellite or rocket
- Medical emergency: a crew member needs urgent assistance
- Computer failure: this can prevent cooling and oxygen production
- Air leak: this can dangerously lower pressure inside the ISS
- Fire: smoke spreads easily through the ventilation system

AVOID THE FALLOUT

STEP 1 Grab your survival kit and get in the car. Close the windows and turn off the air conditioning. Get out of the path of the radiation by travelling at a right angle to the wind direction.

STEP 2 Find a shelter outside the danger zone, preferably one made of concrete. Seal all the windows and air vents with tape and plastic, and turn off the air conditioning and water taps.

When nuclear accidents happen in power plants, dangerous radioactive material may be released into the air and carried over hundreds of kilometres. Here is what you should do if you are in the danger zone.

STEP 3 Only eat food and drink water that is sealed in airtight containers, such as tins and bottles. Flush radioactive materials out of your body by drinking lots of water.

STEP 4 Decontaminate yourself. Take off your clothes and get an adult to burn them. Wash yourself regularly with soap and water that has not been exposed to contaminated air.

STEP 5 Stay in your shelter until you are given the all-clear by rescuers. When you go outside, wear goggles and breathe through a bandana that has been rinsed in water. Use a mirror to attract the attention of the rescuers.

SURVIVAL KIT

- A portable radio for following official updates on radiation levels and the direction of the wind
- Strong sticky tape and thick plastic for sealing up windows and doors
- Food, water and soap in sealed containers
- A change of clothes, goggles, a bandana and a small mirror

SCUBA DRIVING

STEP 1 Wind down your window or break it using a heavy object. Escape through the window if you can, otherwise let the water spill in. You won't be able to open the doors when they are partially submerged because the weight of the water outside will push against them.

STEP 2 While the car fills with water, remove your seat belt. Hold on to the door handle so that you know where it is.

STEP 3 Take slow, deep breaths while there is still air in the car. When the water reaches your neck, take a large gulp of air and hold it.

You're not doomed if the car you are travelling in plunges into water. It will float for a while, so you can simply open the doors and escape. If it sinks before you can do this, follow these steps instead.

STEP 4 Now that the water pressure is the same inside and outside the car, you will be able to open the door. Give it a good shove with your foot while steadying yourself by holding on to your seat.

STEP 5 It is easy to become disorientated under water. If you are not sure which way is 'up', look for air bubbles, as these always rise. If there are no bubbles, breathe out a little to make some yourself.

STEP 6 Push off the car with your feet. As you rise, watch out for things that may injure you, such as rocks or passing boats.

BE PREPARED

- If you travel near water regularly, devise an escape plan and discuss it with your fellow passengers.
- Think about how you would assist less able passengers to escape if your car was submerged.
- At all times, keep tools inside the vehicle for breaking the windows.
- Practise making air bubbles under water when you are in a swimming pool.

SURFACING IN A SUIT

STEP 1 Climb up into the escape chamber. You will need to fill this with water because the escape hatch can't open until the pressure inside the chamber is equal to the sea pressure.

STEP 2 Put on your Submarine Escape Suit and open the water valve to flood the chamber. Use the high-pressure hose to fill the suit's hood with air so you can breathe.

Your submarine has hit rocks and is taking on a lot of water. There isn't enough time to wait for the Deep Submergence Rescue Vehicle, as you need to evacuate immediately – this is what to do.

STEP 3 Swim upwards and out into the sea through the escape hatch. It will have popped open when the pressure in the chamber and the sea pressure equalized.

STEP 4 Close the hatch to make the chamber watertight, so that it can be drained for the next person. Now swim to the surface. The air in your hood will help you to rise in the water.

STEP 5 Use the special pull cord to inflate the insulating layer of your suit with carbon dioxide gas. This is stored in cylinders inside the suit. The inflated layer will keep you warm and afloat while you wait to be picked up by a rescue team.

PRIZ RESCUE

In August 2005, the Russian mini-submarine *Priz* became stuck in nets and cables in the Pacific Ocean near Siberia, Russia. The craft had oxygen supplies for 72 hours only. By the time the UK's Submarine Rescue Service arrived, the submarine had about 12 hours of air left. The rescue team quickly set about cutting the nets and cables using its remotely operated underwater vehicle *Scorpio*, and with about four hours of air remaining, *Priz* finally surfaced.

If you lose track of time and run out of air while you're diving, don't panic and think you've drawn your last breath. These steps will take you to the surface, where you can fill your lungs.

TANKLESS TASK

STEP 1 Let the members of your diving party know that you have run out of air. Perform the universal signal for this by moving your flattened hand from side to side under your chin.

STEP 2 Share a fellow diver's regulator. Lock arms to stay close to each other as you ascend. Pass the regulator back and forth, taking two breaths each time. Exhale while the other diver takes their breaths.

STEP 3 If nobody is in sight, make your way to the surface immediately. Look upwards so that your throat is as straight as it can be, and exhale as you rise.

A rapid ascent from the high-pressure water, at depth, to the lower-pressure water, near the surface, causes 'the bends'. Rise no more than 9m per minute to avoid this fatal illness.

 # BUBBLE TROUBLE

STEP 1 Stop at 9m intervals to check the time. If you have taken less than a minute to travel 9m, hang around until the rest of the minute has passed.

STEP 2 When you are 5m below the surface, stop for 3 minutes. This is a safety measure that makes up for any miscalculations in climb times that you may have made on the way up.

STEP 3 Get into a hyperbaric chamber if you surface too quickly. The air in it will be highly pressurized. Breathe oxygen through a mask while an operator reduces the pressure gradually.

STAGES OF THE BENDS

- Nitrogen from the air that you breathe in from the dive tank dissolves in your blood.

- The nitrogen forms gas bubbles in your blood as the pressure on your body reduces rapidly during an over-quick rise. The bubbles obstruct the flow of your blood, causing damage to your organs.

- In the hyperbaric chamber, high-pressure air dissolves the bubbles. They don't re-form when the pressure on your body is reduced gradually.

ABANDON SHIP!

FROM SHIP TO SHORE

STEP 1 Go to your cabin and put on your Personal Floatation Device (PFD). If you packed a survival kit, grab it and then go to your emergency assembly point.

STEP 2 Follow the instructions of the crew members, who will direct you to your life raft. Be patient in the queue to get on it – there is a place on a life raft for everyone.

Seven short blasts, followed by one long blast of a ship's whistle, signal that you must abandon the vessel. Don't jump overboard if you hear this – you can reach dry land without even getting your feet wet.

STEP 3 Take a seat and put on your safety harness. The life raft will be lowered onto the water at a quick but steady speed, and may rock back and forth a bit like a swing.

STEP 4 Help to row the life raft away from the sinking ship. Row as fast as possible so that your vessel is not sucked underwater as the cruise liner sinks.

STEP 5 Put on warm clothing. The life raft's cover will protect you from the sun, wind and rain – but, unless there is heating in the vessel, it could get cold.

STEP 6 Brace yourself for an air-sea rescue! A rescuer will put a looped harness over your head and under your arms, and will accompany you up to the aircraft.

→ BEFORE YOU SET SAIL

- Pack a survival kit.
- Make sure there is a PFD in your cabin. If you can't reach this in an emergency, spare PFDs will be on the decks and in the life rafts.
- Find out the location of the emergency assembly point.

JOLLY DODGER

REPEL ALL BOARDERS!

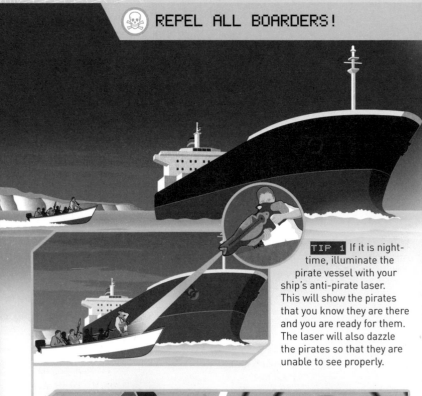

TIP 1 If it is night-time, illuminate the pirate vessel with your ship's anti-pirate laser. This will show the pirates that you know they are there and you are ready for them. The laser will also dazzle the pirates so that they are unable to see properly.

TIP 2 Blast the pirates with a Long-Range Acoustic Device. Don't forget to wear ear protectors, though – it can produce continuous sound at a deafening 162 decibels (dB).

A jet engine produces about 130dB, and sounds of more than 150dB can burst your eardrums! So the noise of your acoustic device will cause most pirates to flee.

Today's pirates don't fly the Jolly Roger or use cutlasses. But they do use small, speedy crafts and the element of surprise to capture ships. Here are the latest ways to escape from modern pirates.

TIP 3 Try shooting jets of seawater at the pirates using the ship's fire hoses. The large fire pumps in the engine room will give you enough pressure to knock the pirates off their feet.

TIP 4 Use the Mobility Denial System. This device sprays a non-poisonous foam that makes any surface too slippery to walk on. Make sure you spray the decks of both vessels.

TIP 5 Whether they are deterred by the noise, water jets or because they can't move about on either of the slippery vessels, the pirates are sure to leave. Radio the authorities with the pirates' direction of travel so that they can be caught.

→ HOW TO AVOID PIRATES

- ⚠ Don't discuss your ship's route or cargo in front of strangers when you are in port.
- ⚠ Search the ship each time you leave port to make sure no one is on board without authorization.
- ⚠ Keep a constant watch in well-known pirate hotspots.

LOST AT SEA

TIP 1 Collect rainwater in any type of vessel you have, such as an empty drinks can, or even your shoe. Don't drink seawater. This can cause kidney failure, which can be fatal.

TIP 2 Avoid paddling in circles by checking your direction of travel regularly using a compass or the stars. You won't escape the open sea if you stay in the same area of water.

HOW YOU COULD BE LOST AT SEA

- 🏃 You have abandoned a sinking ship.
- 🏃 Pirates have taken your ship.
- 🏃 A storm set your vessel off course and you are disorientated.
- 🏃 You escaped from a desert island on a self-made raft.
- 🏃 You were carried out to sea on a pedalo.

With nothing but water in every direction, it is easy to understand how people can get lost at sea. Don't worry if this happens to you. There are simple things that you can do to get out of this situation.

TIP 3 Look for signs of land, such as birds and cumulus clouds. Birds tend to fly towards land at night and away from it during the day. Cumulus clouds are flat, puffy clouds that sit low in the sky and usually form over land.

TIP 4 Keep a lookout for passing ships or aeroplanes. Signal to them for help using flares or mirrors, or by waving your arms. You should also signal to any land that you see. You never know, somebody might spot you and raise the alarm.

TIP 5 When you find land, look for a suitable landing point, such as a gently sloping beach, and aim for it. Paddle hard to avoid being capsized or turned sideways by a large, oncoming wave. Use a breaker (above) to carry you ashore by riding on it.

TIP 6 Always make landfall in daylight. There are many hazards on the coast, such as rocks, cliffs and coral reefs. You may fail to spot them in the dark.

 # NATURAL HAZARDS

You can fall foul of nature wherever you are – whether it be the city, a rural area or the great outdoors. A bit of knowledge and common sense will help you to escape most natural hazards. When disasters or extraordinary weather strike, evacuation is usually the best option. If you get stranded in a wild and remote place, you'll need basic survival, navigation and signalling skills. Dealing with an animal requires an understanding of how that animal thinks and behaves, and what its weak points are.

ISLAND GETAWAY

TIP 1 While you still have battery power, check your mobile phone for a signal. If you manage to make a call, rescuers will work with your phone company to pinpoint your exact location. All you need to do is relax and enjoy the island while you wait for the rescue party to arrive.

TIP 2 Think survival! This means finding water and food. If there is no fresh water available, wrap rags around your feet and lower legs, and walk through long grass at dawn. The rags will absorb dew from the plants. Wring this water into a container, then drink it.

Finding yourself washed up on a sunny desert island with sandy beaches may not seem like a bad thing at first. However, you will soon miss your friends and luxuries, so signal for help as soon as you can.

TIP 3 Make a shelter. Build it in a place where you can spot potential rescue planes and ships easily. Use tree branches for the frame and palm leaves for the cover.

TIP 4 Light three fires in a triangle or in a line. These are international distress signals. During the day, throw on rubber items, such as shoes, to create dark smoke.

TIP 5 Use driftwood or rocks to create shapes on the beach. These should attract the attention of passing aeroplanes. Just make sure that they are visible from the air.

TIP 6 Signal to passing ships and planes using a shiny piece of metal. Catch sunlight on the metal and direct the light towards the craft.

MAKING FIRE

🔧 You will need:
Bow: a shoelace and a long stick
Drill: a shorter stick
Socket: a large shell
Fire board: a piece of timber with a V-shaped notch cut into an edge

🔧 1) Put dry grass into the V-shaped notch. 2) Wrap the bow string once around the drill and then put one end of the drill next to the notch. 3) Push the socket onto the other end of the drill while moving the bow back and forth. 4) When smoke rises from the grass, blow on it to make a flame.

Worried about falling into quicksand? It's impossible to sink in over your head – but if you do find yourself in it up to your waist, follow these steps to get out.

① SINK OR SWIM

STEP 1 Don't struggle, move as slowly as possible. And don't let anyone pull you out. The force needed to lift your foot out is the same force needed to lift a medium-sized car.

STEP 2 Ask someone to pour water around you. This might help loosen that deadly, sucking mixture of sand, clay and salt water. Remember to stay calm, panicking will make things worse.

STEP 1 If the alligator chomps on one of your limbs, punch it on the snout. This will make it open its mouth. You must escape the beast's grip before it starts to spin its body into a death roll. If it does this, you will be shaken like a doll until the alligator has torn off a chunk of you.

✚ SEE YOU LATER ALLIGATOR

Alligators are not usually aggressive towards humans, but you could come across one that is particularly hungry and willing to attack. Make sure that you don't end up as its lunch!

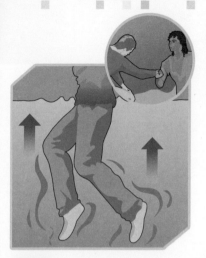

STEP 3 Wriggle your legs. The water will flow into the space created and loosen the sand. Hold somebody's hand for support as you slowly work your way upwards and out of the quicksand.

GET KARTA

An orangutan named Karta made an ingenious break for freedom from Australia's Adelaide Zoo in 2009. The clever ape used a stick to tangle wires and short-circuit the electric fence around her enclosure. She then piled up branches and other items from her enclosure against a wall to make a ramp, which she clambered up to escape. The entire zoo was evacuated, but after less than an hour of wandering around, Karta decided to head back home all by herself!

STEP 2 Run away – fast! These creatures don't like to run for too long or to stray too far from the water. If you are reasonably fit, you can outrun an alligator – they have a top speed of about 18km/h, while the average child can sprint at around 21km/h.

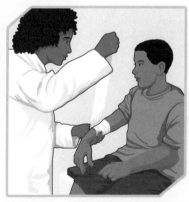

STEP 3 Seek medical attention immediately, even for small cuts. An alligator's mouth contains micro-organisms, called pathogens, that can cause deadly infections if they get into your bloodstream and remain there untreated.

LOST IN THE JUNGLE

YOUR WAY OUT OF A FOREST

TIP 1 Thrash through thick vegetation using a stick. Watch out for creatures lurking in the undergrowth! There are many poisonous animals in the jungle, such as snakes and spiders.

TIP 2 Wherever you can, make a path linking natural breaks in the vegetation. You will save energy if you do as little thrashing as possible.

JUNGLE JULIANE

On 24 December 1971, Juliane Koepcke woke up in a jungle in Peru strapped to a seat from the plane that she had been travelling in. The plane had exploded during a storm. Juliane followed a stream downhill for ten days until she came across a hut, where she took shelter. Three lumberjacks arrived the next day and helped Juliane to complete her jungle escape.

Dense foliage, twisting vines and thick roots that sit above the ground make jungles very difficult to navigate, and easy to get lost in. If you lose your way in a leafy labyrinth, these tips will help you to escape.

TIP 3 Keep a close eye on the ground. You might find a track that has been made by other humans. It may lead you to a village where you can get help.

TIP 4 Plan a downhill route. It should pass tall features that are visible from the ground most of the time. The landmarks will keep you on track and stop you travelling in circles.

TIP 5 Leave a trail for rescuers. Snap off branches at eye-level regularly along your route. It will be obvious to rescuers that the breaks were made by a person, so these will help the team track you down.

TIP 6 Build a fire in a clearing. Fan the flames with wet palm leaves to create smoke signals.

TIP 7 Look for a river and travel downhill beside it. Rivers often lead to villages and towns.

Most mosquito bites are harmless, but some can be deadly – certain mosquitoes carry diseases that they pass on to humans when they bite them. Avoid mosquito bites by using these tips.

DEADLY BITE

TIP 1 Spray yourself, and any clothing that you plan to wear, with insect repellent. Repellents block chemical sensors on the mosquitoes' antennae, making it difficult for them to detect you.

TIP 2 Wear light colours. They keep you cooler than dark colours. Mosquitoes are drawn to the heat of your body and lactic acid in your sweat, so you can avoid bites by staying cool.

STEP 1 Run for cover. Killer bees will pursue you for up to 1.5km, which is much further than any other bee will. If you can, run into the wind, as this will help you to outpace the bees. You may be tempted to swat them as you run – don't! This will make the bees angrier and more determined to sting you.

BUZZ OFF!

The killer bees of the Americas are aggressive and quick to attack. If you are likely to come across them, make a beeline for the steps here so that you don't get stung.

TIP 3 Sleep under a mosquito net. It lets in air but it is too tightly woven for mosquitoes to get through. Avoid lying against the net because mosquitoes could bite you through it. Check the net for holes regularly.

MOZZIE HOTSPOTS

🦟 Stagnant water: mosquitoes lay their eggs on the surface of the water.

🦟 Tall grasses and shrubs: adult mosquitoes take refuge from daytime heat in the shade provided by the plants.

🦟 Compost: mosquitoes are attracted to the carbon dioxide emitted during the decomposition of organic material. The heat released during this process also attracts mosquitoes.

STEP 2 Protect your face and head as you run. Killer bees prefer to attack these parts of your body, so pull your shirt or another piece of clothing over them, or use your arms. Try not to slow down your running as you do this.

STEP 3 Take shelter in a building, tent or any type of structure that will keep out the bees. Don't jump into water. Killer bees will hang around until you come up for air and will attack when you surface.

The South American river you are about to cross may be full of piranhas. These fish can devour an animal in seconds. Here is how to keep the flesh on your bones.

THE BAIT ESCAPE

STEP 1 Test the temperature of the water. It might be too cold for piranhas – they don't like temperatures below 24°C. If the reading is lower than this, you are free to cross, but watch out for strong currents!

STEP 2 If the river temperature is suitable for piranhas, assume they are there. Create a diversion by throwing bait, such as another type of fish, into the water downstream from where you plan to cross. While the fish are distracted, you can make your move. Follow the advice in Step 3 if the piranhas strip the carcass too quickly and you need to backtrack.

STEP 3 Cross the river at night-time while the piranhas are asleep. Don't talk or splash as you go, otherwise you will disturb them. Beware of nocturnal predators, such as caimans!

An anaconda is coiled around you. It has no venom, but it can squeeze the life out of you using a pressure equivalent to a female elephant sitting on your chest. So act quickly!

EASE THE SQUEEZE

STEP 1 Don't exhale your breath. If you do, this will allow the snake to squeeze tighter. You won't be able to get your breath back and eventually you won't be able to breathe at all.

STEP 2 Grab the end of the anaconda's tail and unwind the creature's coiled body, pulling it away as you go. If you can't reach the snake's tail, begin at the head.

STEP 3 If the anaconda's grip is too strong and you are unable to unravel it, your only option is to hit it on the head. Keep doing this until the snake releases you.

AVOIDING ANACONDAS

- Stay out of shallow rivers and swamps in the Amazon region of South America. This is where anacondas live.

- Make noise to let anacondas know you are about, as they are not usually keen to meet you either.

- If you see that an anaconda is following you and flicking its tongue to smell and track you, it may be planning to attack. Get away – fast!

You fell into a fast-flowing river and the current is dragging you towards the top of a waterfall. Don't just go with the flow – there are things you can do to avoid the perilous plunge.

RAGING RIVER

STEP 1 Go with the current, but swim sideways towards the bank. If you try to swim upstream against the current you will get tired, increasing the chances of you drowning or ending up at the bottom of the falls.

STEP 2 If the bank is too high and you can't get out, grab an overhanging tree branch. Shout for help as loudly as you can so that passers-by hear you above the sound of the water.

STEP 3 Hang on tight and wait for the rescue boat to arrive. Let go only when a rescuer tells you to. After you are hauled aboard, you will be wrapped in blankets and whisked back to dry land.

HOW TO AVOID AN UNPLANNED DIP

- Stay clear of wet, slippery rocks and muddy banks.
- Watch out for unstable banks that could give way.
- Use a bridge instead of wading across a river.
- Don't stand up in a rowing boat. You might cause it to capsize.

Hippos defend their territory aggressively and you've just invaded one accidentally while taking a safari walk. So, how do you deal with the angry, two-tonne hippo charging at you?

HOP IT FROM A HIPPO

STEP 1 Run away in a zig-zagging line. Hippos can run at up to 48km/h, which is much faster than you can, but their bulk makes them less agile, so they are much slower than you at changing direction.

STEP 2 Run among trees or rocks. The hippo's size will make it difficult for the animal to dodge and weave through these obstacles.

STEP 3 Race to the safari tour jeep and jump into it. Shut the door behind you as quickly as you can. The hippo may charge at the door, but it will give up when it realizes it can't get to you.

HIPPO AWARENESS

- If you are in a boat, allow hippos in the water plenty of space.
- Tap the side of the boat to let hippos under the water know you are around so one doesn't come up beneath you.
- Avoid thickets where hippos may be hiding.
- Listen out for oxpecker birds – they live alongside hippos.

HOTFOOT IT FROM A DESERT

ESCAPE UNSCORCHED

STEP 1 Create a ground-to-air distress signal using rocks. You may think the chances of a light aircraft passing overhead are small, but you might get lucky.

STEP 2 Leave a note in the jeep for anybody who might spot the abandoned car. Write down the date and time you left and your direction of travel.

STEP 3 Stay in the shade during the hottest part of the day. If you don't, the sun will sap your energy. Overhangs in rocks make ideal shelters from the sun.

The blistering desert temperatures have caused the jeep's engine to overheat. Nobody knows you are missing, so there is little chance of a search being launched. You'll just have to escape on foot.

STEP 4 Search for water. Cacti are a good source. They store it in their fleshy part, called the pith. Slice out pieces of it and suck out the juice. Take an extra supply for your journey, as there is a chance you might not come across any more water sources along your escape route.

STEP 5 Find the direction you should be travelling in by orienting yourself and your map north. North of the equator you can find where north is using the North Star. South of the equator, use the Southern Cross constellation to find south first – north is in the opposite direction.

STEP 6 Travel on ridges wherever it is possible so that you can spot desert towns in the distance. Don't be tempted to hike to one during the day. Wait until the sun sets before you go on any long journeys.

STELLAR ADVICE

- To find the North Star in the night sky, mentally draw a line through the two lowest stars in the Ursa Major constellation – this is the one that looks like a saucepan if you join the dots.

- Extend the line upwards until it meets a star that is brighter than the ones around it. This is the North Star.

- Draw an imaginary line straight down from it to see where north is on the ground.

Desert winds can kick up sandstorms that blow at up to 130km/h. If one of them is heading your way, take steps to avoid being sandblasted or suffocated by it.

🔘 SAND HASSLE

STEP 1 Cover up! Put on a long-sleeved top and trousers. Moisten a piece of cloth and then wrap it around your nose and mouth to protect your airways.

STEP 2 Use any shelter you can find, such as a boulder. Sit on the side facing away from the oncoming wind to shield yourself from the full force of the storm.

The weather outside is boiling hot. You are constantly tired and thirsty, and sweating all the time. Don't melt down. Keep your cool and chill out instead.

🔘 BEAT THE HEAT

STEP 1 If you can, stay indoors during the hours of 10am to 4pm. This is when the sun is usually the strongest. Lower the temperature in your home by opening the windows and closing the curtains. Switch on a fan if you have one.

WHAT TO DO IF A HEATWAVE IS COMING

- Cancel any strenuous activities that you had planned.
- Get lots of sunscreen. One with an SPF number rating of 30 or more is best.
- Check to make sure your air conditioning or fan is working.
- Stock up on bottled water in case there is a drought or the waterpipes burst in the heat and the supply is cut off.

STEP 2 Wear a long-sleeved top, hat and sunglasses when you are outside. These help to protect you from ultraviolet light in the sun's rays. This light can burn your skin and damage your eyes.

STEP 3 Drink lots of water. When you sweat, your body loses water that it needs to work properly. Don't wait until you are thirsty – drinking before then keeps the water levels in your body from dropping too low.

STEP 4 Apply sunscreen regularly. Use one with a high SPF rating. The letters stand for sun protection factor. The higher the number rating, the longer you can stay in the sun without burning.

STEP 5 Have a picnic in the shade with your friends instead of playing sport. Your body struggles to cool itself fast enough when you exercise in the sun, making you tired.

STEP 6 Take breaks in the shade often, especially if you are outside during the hottest part of the day. Use an umbrella to create shade in places where there is none.

MOUNTAIN RANGING

STEP 1 Find a high point from which you can get a good view of the mountainside. Use your binoculars to find a stream that you can follow downhill to a bridge or rail line.

STEP 2 Fix your compass on the direction of the stream (see p.105). The instrument will help you to find your target, even if you have to walk through a forest to get to it.

If you get lost while hiking in the mountains, phone for help, keep warm and wait to be rescued. Only attempt the following steps if you fail to make contact with rescuers and nobody knows you are lost.

STEP 3 Check your compass regularly so that you stay on course. Mark your trail using tree branches – you never know, somebody might spot them and come to your aid.

PEAK PRECAUTIONS

- Never go hiking in mountains on your own.

- Let people know that you are going on a trek, and tell them where you are going and what time you plan to be back. If you don't return by that time, they will know to raise the alarm.

- Keep a compass and map with you at all times.

- Take along a survival kit (see p.104), which should contain warm and waterproof clothing, as well as food and water.

STEP 4 When you reach the stream, make a rock marker. If you are turning left, put a small rock to the left of a larger one, and another small rock on top of it (see above). A rock on the right-hand side would show you have turned right.

STEP 5 If you come to a rail bridge, stop and wait for a train to come along. Wave your arms to catch the driver's attention and shout loudly for help, then stay put – the driver will tell the rescue services where to find you.

A grizzly bear has wandered into your campsite. What do you do? You certainly don't run – the bear can run much faster than you. Do these things instead.

BEAR NECESSITIES

STEP 1 Stand tall and make yourself look bigger by waving your arms. You could lift your backpack over your head. Keep still if the bear charges at you. It is probably bluffing and will turn and go if you stand your ground.

STEP 2 If the bear persists, use your pepper spray. Point the spray at its eyes and release the contents. This will either disorientate the bear so you can make your escape, or put it off attacking you.

STEP 3 Play dead if the bear makes contact with you. Lie flat on the ground to protect your body's vital organs and cover your head with your hands. Stay like this for several minutes after the bear leaves.

BEAR BASICS

- If you see a bear in the distance, leave the area.
- Bears generally want to avoid meeting you, so let them know that you are in their territory by singing or talking loudly.
- Store food in bear-proof containers to prevent a hungry bear from smelling it.

Seeing a mountain lion in the wild is an awesome experience. But get too close, and things could turn nasty. Remember these steps if you come face to face with a mountain lion.

🐾 ESCAPE CLAWS

STEP 1 Look the mountain lion in the eye and make yourself appear bigger, for example by opening out your jacket. Give the lion plenty of room to escape.

STEP 2 Snarl and growl at the lion as you back away slowly. Resist the temptation to run off, as the lion's natural hunting instinct will kick in and it will chase you down.

STEP 3 Make the lion retreat if it is about to attack by tossing items from your pockets at it. Don't bend down to pick up weapons – you will look like four-legged prey to the lion.

DON'T CAVE IN!

GETTING YOU OUT OF A HOLE

STEP 1 Put on extra clothing – you will be in these cold and damp conditions longer than you had planned. Ration food and drinks to make them last longer.

STEP 2 See if your mobile phone has a signal. If there isn't one, turn off the phone to conserve its energy. Try it again at intervals.

STEP 3 Your group should use one light only at a time, and only when the group is moving, or when light is needed to perform a task.

Caves are exciting places to explore, but if you get lost in them, you soon find out how cold, wet and maze-like they are. Don't lose heart if this happens to you, these steps will guide you to the light at the end of the tunnel.

STEP 4 Light a candle to see if air is coming in from an opening to the outside. The incoming flow of air will bend the flame in one direction. Travel in the opposite direction to find the way out.

STEP 5 At every junction, make an arrow with rocks to indicate the direction that you are taking. Not only will this tell rescuers where you have gone, it will also prevent you from backtracking.

STEP 6 Keep the incoming air on your face and look for light. Like the airflow, the light is coming in from the outside. The brighter the cave gets, the closer you are to your exit.

CAVING KIT

- 🔸 Wellington boots, an undersuit made of synthetic fibres and a waterproof outer layer. Take along extra clothes.
- 🔸 Caving helmet – with a working light.
- 🔸 Food and drinks, such as high-energy bars and water.
- 🔸 Candles – for use as an emergency light source, and for testing for incoming air.

HORSE JUMPING

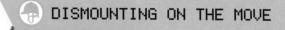

DISMOUNTING ON THE MOVE

STEP 1 Kick out both of your feet from the stirrups – you don't want to get stuck in them on the way off.

STEP 2 Move your hands into the dismount position. If you plan to dismount on the left side of the horse, place your right hand on the front of the saddle, and your left hand on the back of the horse's lower neck. Do the opposite if you have to get off on the other side.

THINGS THAT MAKE A HORSE BOLT

- Loud noises, including the sound of a car's horn and an engine backfiring.
- Unexpected movement, such as a plastic bag blowing along the ground.
- Overly tightened saddles, mouth bits and bridles.
- The horse doesn't want to be ridden.

Horses can sometimes bolt, even when there is a rider in the saddle. If your horse does run away out of control, it is best to hold on until the animal calms down. However, sometimes an emergency dismount is the only option.

STEP 3 Bend your body forwards and press your hands downwards while you kick your leg high over the animal's rear. Lift your right leg for a left-hand dismount, and your left one if you are getting off on the right.

STEP 4 Bring your legs together, let go of the reins and push away from the saddle. Aim to land at a right angle to the horse – you won't fall under the animal from this position if you lose your balance.

STEP 5 Bend your knees as you land. If you keep your legs straight, your knees will take a force equal to five times your body weight. Bend them and they won't bear all this force – other areas of your legs will help to absorb the shock.

STEP 6 Move away from the horse's back legs in case it tries to kick you. When it does slow down, approach it slowly while speaking in a low, calm voice. The horse won't understand what you are saying, but it will be soothed by the sound.

If you crash land in the Arctic, don't wander off to find help. Even if you could survive the cold, the nearest town may be thousands of kilometres away. Get rescuers to come to you!

❄ LOST AT THE POLE

STEP 1 Signal for help by forming an SOS shape on the ground with any items you have to hand. If the aircraft's radio works, call for help on channel 121.5MHz – this is the band reserved for aircraft in distress.

STEP 2 Heat snow to make drinking water. Don't eat snow, as it will make your body colder. Your body would also use a lot of energy to melt the snow, making you need more water, so you would end up dehydrated.

STEP 3 Use the aircraft as a shelter until the helicopter rescue team arrives. Switch between huddling together and exercising to keep warm. Although exercising creates warmth, don't exhaust yourself doing it.

Glaciers are criss-crossed with cracks, called crevasses. These can plunge deep into the ice, but the one you've fallen into is fairly shallow. Now, let's get you out of there!

SLIP THROUGH THE CRACK

STEP 1 Shout for help. Stay in one place as you do this – there are cracks in the ground all around you and another fall would take you deeper into the glacier.

STEP 2 Keep warm while you wait to be rescued. Do this by exercising in one spot as often as you can, and curling up in a ball on the ground when you are tired.

STEP 3 If you are alone, your only hope is to move along the bottom of the crevasse to see if you can find a way out – some lead out to the side of the glacier.

GLACIER HINTS

- Never travel across a glacier on your own.
- Always rope yourself to other members of your party, so if you fall into a crevasse, you can be pulled up to safety.
- Probe the ice with your ski pole to see if it is solid.
- If you use a snow bridge to cross a crevasse, crawl on it so that you spread your weight as much as possible.

Stay put if you get stranded in a car during a blizzard. The car will protect you from the strong winds and driving snow. It's your job to fend off the intense cold and get rescued.

❄ WHITEOUT

STEP 1 Phone for help. While you wait for it to arrive, the engine can be turned on at intervals to power the heating, but keep the exhaust pipe clear of snow, and open a window slightly, to avoid being poisoned by exhaust fumes.

TIP 1 As well as layers of warm clothing, always wear a hat, gloves and insulated boots in freezing temperatures. Ideally, you should also wear a balaclava. Frostbite can affect any part of the body, but your hands, feet, ears, nose and lips are the most vulnerable to it.

⊖ FROSTBITE

Temperatures below zero can cause frostbite. You can lose fingers and toes to this skin-freezing condition, but these tips will help you to take the bite out of the frost.

STEP 2 Make the car more visible in the thick snow. Keep on the headlights. And hang the high-visibility jacket from your car's emergency travel kit, or a brightly coloured piece of plastic or cloth, from a window on the traffic side of the car.

STEP 3 When the heating is off, exercise to keep warm. Stomp your feet and clap your hands for about two minutes every 15 minutes. If you still feel cold, put an item of clothing on top of your head. Stay positive – the rescue services will find you!

TIP 2 Wrinkle your face to stop it from freezing. Check yourself and others regularly for the early signs of frostbite: waxy, white patches. Seek medical attention immediately if you spot some.

TIP 3 Keep active if you are outside. The best way to stay warm and avoid frostbite is by exercising. But pace yourself and don't overdo it, or you'll use energy that your body needs to fight the cold.

AVALANCHE!

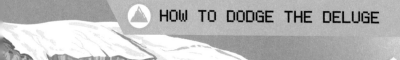

TIP 1 If the avalanche starts right below your feet, jump upslope beyond the fracture. This is the crack that forms when the avalanche pulls away from snow higher up the slope.

TIP 2 Set off your emergency avalanche rescue beacon. This signals your location to rescuers.

TIP 3 Ski at a right angle to the avalanche. You may be able to get out of its path before it reaches you.

If an avalanche is coming your way, don't try to ski ahead of it like James Bond – it could be moving at 150km/h. The tips here won't make you an action hero, but pay attention and you may live to ski another day.

TIP 4 The snow acts a bit like water when it is moving, so swim as hard as you can to stay on top of it. Keep your head up as you do this.

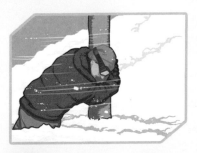

TIP 5 Grab onto a tree or boulder. Even if you get pulled away from it, the worst part of the avalanche will have gone past you.

TIP 6 If you get buried by the snow, hold your hands in front of your nose and mouth to create an air-filled space for breathing.

TIP 7 Use your snow shovel to dig your way out. Dribble to work out which way is up. Dig in the opposite direction to your dribble.

SAFETY CHECKS

- Listen out for a 'whomp' sound. It means the snow is unstable.
- Look for long cracks in the snow.
- Avalanches occur more often on slopes of between 35° and 45°.
- Slopes covered by wind-blown snow are more dangerous than slopes that are eroded (worn away) by the wind.

ICE BREAKER

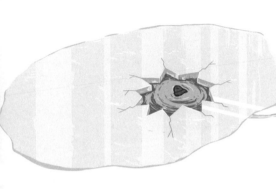

STEP 1 Look up for the hole that you made when you crashed into the water – this area will appear darker than the ice. Kick off your skis and swim towards the hole.

STEP 2 When you surface, turn and face the point at which you entered the water. You should get out here, as you know the ice beyond it has supported your weight already.

You lost control while skiing and have just taken an icy plunge into a frozen lake. Before cold shock gets the better of you and you can't function properly, let's get you out of your ice bath and into a warm one.

STEP 3 Stretch your arms over the ice and dig safety picks into it. Stab the ice with the picks hand over hand while propelling yourself out of the water by kicking your legs up and down.

STEP 4 Roll away from the hole. By doing this you will spread your weight over the largest area possible. Follow the route you came in and don't stand up until you are back on solid ground.

STEP 5 Warm up, even if you don't feel particularly cold. Remove all your wet clothes, wrap yourself in a blanket and have a tepid drink before taking a warm bath.

RESCUING A VICTIM OF THE ICE

- Resist the urge to run up to the hole to rescue the victim.
- Call the emergency services.
- While you remain on the bank, throw one end of a rope to the victim and ask them to tie it around themselves.
- Try to pull them towards the bank. If you can't, hold on to the rope until the emergency services arrive.

VOLCANIC ERUPTION

STEP 1 Tune into official reports on the radio to find out the wind direction. This will help you to predict the movement of the ash and poisonous gases. Bear in mind this information when you choose your escape route.

STEP 2 As you evacuate the area, keep clear of flying rocks by putting a hill or mountain between you and the volcano. The scorching-hot rocks, which can travel at speeds of up to 1,458km/h, have been known to kill people and set buildings on fire.

An erupting volcano looks impressive, but don't hang around to enjoy the spectacle. As well as lava, volcanoes can emit suffocating ash, poisonous gases and red-hot rocks that shoot into the air.

STEP 3 Avoid the poisonous gases. They are heavier than air and will stay low to the ground, so keep off it and get as high as you can.

STEP 4 Make yourself a respirator to filter out the ash and gases. To do this, simply wet a scarf and wrap it around your nose and mouth.

STEP 5 Find a shelter that is out of the way of the flying rocks. Mountainsides are often dotted with emergency shelters for hikers and you may discover one.

STEP 6 Get inside and stay there until the authorities tell you it is safe to leave. Cover the bottom of the doors with cloth to prevent the ash and gases getting into the building.

ERUPTION HAZARDS

- Lava – the speed varies but it can be up to 56km/h.
- Flying rocks with temperatures of up to 1,000°C.
- Ash that travels on the wind for thousands of kilometres.
- Poisonous gases, including sulphur dioxide and hydrogen sulphide.

Underwater earthquakes can trigger a series of giant waves, called a tsunami. These huge walls of water flatten any coast that they strike, so react quickly if they are surging your way.

TSUNAMI

STEP 1 Race inland and scramble to high, solid ground. Stay put for at least 24 hours. The first wave is not the only one you can expect. It will pull back and may be followed by three or four more waves, which could be even bigger.

STEP 2 If you cannot escape the waves, climb the stairs to the top floor of a tall building. Don't use the lift as it will get stuck if the flood causes a power cut.

STEP 3 Climb a tree if there are no buildings around. Tie yourself to it and cling on as the tsunami passes. If you get swept away, protect your head with one arm and use the other to grab on to something that floats.

WARNING SIGNS

- ⚠ An earthquake strikes relatively close to the coastal area where you are.

- ⚠ Water withdraws quickly and unexpectedly from the beach.

- ⚠ The sea becomes rough very suddenly.

- ⚠ You hear a roaring sound similar to the one made by a jet aeroplane.

- ⚠ Animals are behaving strangely and heading inland.

STEP 1 Get on to the roof of your home to give yourself the best chance of being spotted by rescuers. Tie yourself to the chimney so that you don't fall off. Don't stay inside – you could get trapped by the rising water.

STEP 2 If it becomes clear that the rescue services won't get to you before the water covers the roof, escape on a makeshift raft. Inflatable beds are ideal for this. Paddle to safety using a shovel.

💧 HIGH AND DRY

Heavy rainfall over a short period of time can cause floods that turn a street into a river in a matter of minutes. Here's what to do if your home is swamped by one of these flash floods.

A rip current is a narrow band of fast-moving water that pulls away from the shore. It can carry even the best swimmers out to sea, but there are ways to escape the grip of a rip.

◉ GOING WITH THE FLOW

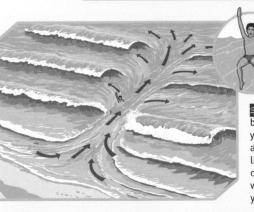

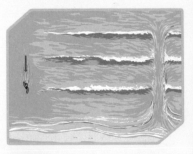

STEP 1 Float on your back or tread water while you wave one arm to attract the attention of the lifeguards. You will get carried out to sea, but you won't go too far before you are rescued.

STEP 2 If you are a strong and confident swimmer, you can get yourself back to the shore. The first thing you must do is make your way out of the side of the current by swimming parallel to the beach.

STEP 3 When you no longer feel the pull of the rip current, swim directly back to shore. The waves will help you to get there.

◯ LIFE SAVER

- ✪ If you are on the beach, toss something that floats to the person in distress and encourage them to go with the current.
- ✪ Alert the lifeguards.
- ✪ If you are in the water, stay a safe distance from others caught in the current – they may panic and pull you under the water.

WHIRLPOOL WISE

- Ocean whirlpools are created by the rise and fall of tides, tsunami and earthquakes.
- There are whirlpools in rivers and at the bottom of certain waterfalls.
- Some whirlpools have a downward pull, known as a vortex.
- Whirlpools in the sea can be up to 75m in diameter.
- The currents in ocean whirlpools move at speeds of up to 28km/h.

STEP 1 Tread water or hang on to a floating object, if there is one around. This gives you a chance to catch your breath and get ready for a tough swim out of the spinning pool.

STEP 2 Swim with the current while moving out of the whirlpool in a diagonal line. Save energy by making long strokes with your arms and fluttering kicks with your legs.

⊕ IN A SPIN

You are caught in a swirling body of water, known as whirlpool, which is dragging you around in circles. Give these steps a whirl before the situation spirals out of control.

Shark attacks are not as common as the movies would have you believe. But if a shark tries to make you its catch of the day, here's how you can be 'the one that got away'.

SHIRK A SHARK

STEP 1 Keep an eye on the shark at all times. If it starts to circle you, it is planning to strike. Don't panic and flail around if it does this – it is in a shark's nature to attack things that are thrashing about.

STEP 2 Shout in the water. The shark won't like the sound. Sharks are attracted to rapid, low-frequency pulsing sounds because fish make them when they flap in the water as they die.

STEP 3 Show the shark that you mean business. If it attacks you, punch it on the gills or poke it in the eyes – these are the only vulnerable areas on a shark's body. When it leaves, swim ashore backwards so that you can watch the shark and know if it comes back.

A giant octopus just grabbed you with one of its sucker-lined arms and more are coming at you from all directions. You wanted a close look at the sealife, but not this close!

OUT OF ARMS' WAY

STEP 1 Pull away as hard as you can. The octopus may give up and let you go because these animals get tired easily. Their blood is a poor carrier of oxygen – most animals use this to convert food into the energy they need to do things.

STEP 2 Turn somersaults. This action should peel you away from the suckers. The pressure from these can tear off flesh – and there are 240 of them on each arm! It's lucky you are wearing a wetsuit.

STEP 3 Swim to the surface as soon as you escape the octopus's grip. It won't follow you up there because it can't breathe air and it doesn't like the light from the sun.

RUN FOR COVER!

STEP 1 Get yourself to a tornado shelter or the basement of a building. These windowless underground rooms will protect you from the storm.

STEP 2 If you are caught outside and there isn't a shelter nearby, try to get out of the path of the tornado by running at a right angle to it. Don't attempt to outrun it.

Tornadoes, also known as twisters, bring swirling winds of more than 200km/h. These dramatic storms leave a trail of destruction behind them. They happen very quickly, so be prepared to act fast if one strikes.

STEP 3 Find a ditch or hollow in the ground. Curl up and cover your head with your arms to protect it from falling debris.

STEP 4 When you leave your shelter after the tornado has passed, avoid the wreckage. Be particularly careful around fallen power lines. These could still be live and you could get a fatal electric shock from them.

STEP 5 Phone the emergency services for help. Remember to stay away from buildings when you use your mobile phone. It could spark any gas that might be leaking.

EARLY WARNINGS

- Cats and dogs start to behave strangely, and birds disappear.
- You hear a waterfall-like sound that turns into a roar as it gets closer to you.
- The sky suddenly turns a greenish-black colour.
- Hailstones begin to fall.
- Clouds start to move across the sky very fast, possibly twisting into a cone shape as they go.
- Debris, such as tree branches and leaves, drop from the sky.

CHEAT LIGHTNING

TIP 1 Lightning is attracted to tall objects, so leave open areas where you are the tallest thing around. Drop metal items immediately, as they could conduct electricity to you.

TIP 2 Stay clear of trees and tall metal structures. If they are struck, the electricity could jump to you, or it could reach you as it spreads away from them through the ground.

70

If you can hear thunder, you are within about 16km of an electrical storm, and there is a chance that you could get struck by lightning. Be a bright spark and read these tips so that you don't have a shocking experience.

TIP 3 Make yourself as small as possible if you are caught in the open. Crouch down and lift your heels off the ground so that very little of you is touching it.

FACTS IN A FLASH

- A bolt of lightning contains up to 1 billion volts of electricity. Each bolt is five times hotter than the surface of the Sun.

- Lightning takes the shortest path to the ground. Tall objects, such as trees and pylons, act like raised ground, which is why lightning heads for them.

- Metal is a good conductor of electricity. This means that the electric current in lightning flows through it easily.

TIP 4 Don't use a landline phone and stop others from using one. Lightning could strike the cables outside and the electricity may flow through them to the phone.

TIP 5 Take refuge in a car. If the car is struck, the current will jump from the metal frame to the ground. Be careful not to touch any metal inside the car.

BEAT THE BLAZE

MAKING A BREAK FOR IT

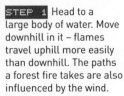

STEP 1 Head to a large body of water. Move downhill in it – flames travel uphill more easily than downhill. The paths a forest fire takes are also influenced by the wind.

FIRE STARTERS

- Lightning strikes are the cause of most natural fires.
- In very high temperatures, certain plants, such as conifers and eucalyptus trees, can burst into flames naturally.
- Sparks can leap from campfires and ignite dry leaves.
- Campfires that aren't put out properly can get out of control.
- Arsonists start fires deliberately.

Forest fires are dangerously unpredictable. The roaring walls of flames can change direction rapidly, and embers can fly off and start new fires. Knowing how to escape a forest fire could be a matter of life and death.

STEP 2 If you can't get to water, use a tree branch to dig a fire break. The hollow causes a break in the line of flames when it passes – the flames can't burn what isn't there.

STEP 3 Lie face down in the trench and cover yourself with your coat. The layer of air between you and the coat will keep away much of the heat of the passing fire.

STEP 4 Check your clothing for spark burns after the fire has passed. Stamp on the clothes if there are signs of burning.

STEP 5 Head upwind, travelling through fire-charred areas. Flames won't return to these because there is nothing left to burn.

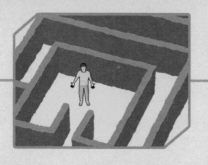

 TRAPPED!

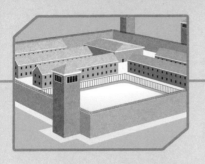

Being trapped in some way doesn't mean there is no way out. You'd be amazed at how easy it is to escape from places or things that are designed to confine or restrain you – read this chapter, and you will see. Sometimes you can be trapped by something that puts your life at risk, such as fire. In these cases you may need to take a dramatic course of action to escape. Even if you must do this, it can be done in a controlled way so that you don't come to any harm.

AMAZING ESCAPES

STEP 1 One way to escape the maze is to use a hedge to guide you out of it. Start off this tactic by placing your left hand on the left-hand hedge.

STEP 2 Keep your hand on the hedge and follow it through the maze. The hedge will lead you to the exit (see above), but you may tour several dead ends before you get there.

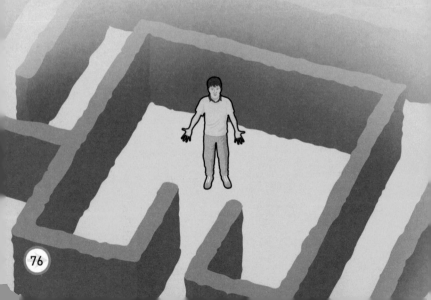

The networks of passages and tall hedges in garden mazes are designed to confuse and disorientate you. If you are trapped in a maze and want to get out, try either of these tactics to get yourself on the right path.

STEP 1 Another way to escape is by dropping a trail of pebbles as you make your way out of the maze. The trail will show you where you have been already.

STEP 2 When you reach a dead-end, turn around and go back. Keep backtracking until you find a route that is not marked by your pebbles, then go along it.

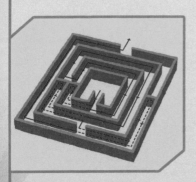

STEP 3 By marking more and more of the maze with the pebbles, you will eventually find yourself at the exit, although this could take some time.

MAZE MONSTER

A mythical beast with a bull's head and a man's body lived in a maze on the island of Crete. The creature, called Minotaur, fed on human flesh. This upset Theseus, a prince from Athens, who went into the maze and killed the monster. Theseus marked his route into the maze with string, which he used to find his way back out again.

PRISON BREAK

STEP 1 Loosen an area of bricks in your cell by scraping out the mortar around them. Carl August Lorentzen used a spoon to do this when he escaped from Horsens State Prison, Denmark, in 1949.

STEP 2 Get rid of any dust and dirt from your cell discreetly. The Great Escape prisoners (see p.79) hid earth from the tunnels that they were digging in bags inside their trouser legs, then scattered it as they walked around.

STEP 3 Find out which times of the day there are the fewest guards on watch, and plan to escape then. The Great Escape prisoners kept logs of the guards' routines.

For as long as there have been prisons, there have been prisoners trying to escape from them. These steps are based on real prison breaks, but it is only fair to warn you that most of the people involved were recaptured.

STEP 4 Alter your prison uniform so people can't tell that you are an escaped convict. In 1945, John Giles walked on to a boat leaving Alcatraz prison, USA, wearing an army uniform stolen from laundry sent to the jail for cleaning.

STEP 5 Squirrel away food for your escape attempt. It is crucial that you keep up your energy levels, as you may have to outrun tracker dogs (see p.91). And you don't know when you will be having your next meal.

STEP 6 When it is time to leave, pull out the loosened bricks, then crawl backwards through the hole. Drag your bed towards you as you go so that it covers your escape route.

THE GREAT ESCAPE

During World War II, a group of prisoners of war took part in an escape from Stalag Luft III, a German prison camp. They dug three tunnels. These were so long that a pumping system had to be made to provide fresh air to the diggers, and there were small rail systems for removing the soil. On 24 March 1944, the escape attempt began. Out of the 76 men who got out, only three avoided capture.

SHAKE THE SHACKLES

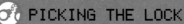

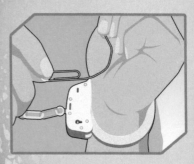

STEP 1 Stretch out one end of the paper clip wire until it is straight. You will use this end to pick the lock.

HANDCUFF KING

Harry Houdini was a highly successful escape artist in the early 1900s. He could free himself from handcuffs, chains, ropes and straitjackets, often while hanging upside down by a rope or even in water. Houdini really enjoyed escaping from handcuffs, and he never encountered a pair from which he couldn't free himself. This earned him the nickname 'The handcuff king'.

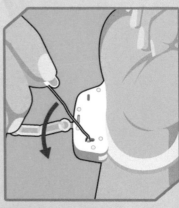

STEP 2 Put the tip of the straightened end of the paper clip into the keyhole. Bend down the paper clip over 90°. You'll see this forms an L-shape at the tip.

Impress your friends by escaping from a pair of handcuffs without using the key. They can be unlocked relatively easily without it – all you need is the know-how and a medium-sized paper clip.

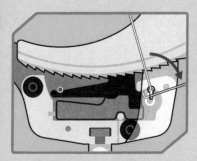

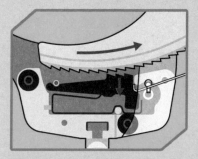

STEP 3 Hook the L-shaped end into the keyhole as shown here in this cutaway of the mechanism. Press down on your tool so that the L-shaped end pushes against the lock (the large black part).

STEP 4 The lock is spring-loaded and will pull away from the jagged teeth in the handcuff bracelet. Now that there is nothing to keep it fixed in place, the bracelet will slide open and you can remove the handcuff.

STEP 5 You may wish to perform the trick with your back to your audience. With practice you will be able to unlock the handcuffs without looking at what you are doing, and you could do the trick under a scarf so that nobody knows how it is done.

STRAIGHT OUT OF THE JACKET

STEP 1 Keep your top arm pressed firmly against you. Then move the hand on your other arm straight up to your shoulder.

SOFIA'S BOUND TO ESCAPE

The straitjacket was designed to restrain somebody who may cause harm to themselves or others. You are not supposed to be able to escape from them, and certainly not as quickly as an English hospital worker called Sofia Romero. On 9 June 2011, she took 4.69 seconds to remove a fastened straitjacket, which is the fastest time anybody has ever done this.

The long sleeves of a straitjacket are tied together behind your back, keeping your arms folded firmly in front of you. A strap between your legs stops the jacket coming off over your head. So, how do you escape?

STEP 2 Lower your head and lift your moving arm over it. You may need to push your head hard through the triangular-shaped gap created by your bent arm, so be careful!

STEP 3 Swing your moving arm down and around to your front. From now on, your arms won't be crossed over each other so it will be easier to move them about.

STEP 4 Push your hands around one side to the buckle that fastens the strap between your legs. Unbuckle it with your fingers through the fabric of the sleeves.

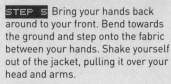

STEP 5 Bring your hands back around to your front. Bend towards the ground and step onto the fabric between your hands. Shake yourself out of the jacket, pulling it over your head and arms.

FIRE ESCAPE

STEP 1 As soon as you are aware of a fire in your home, get out of the burning building immediately. Don't delay by changing out of night clothes or trying to save belongings.

STEP 2 Avoid the suffocating smoke. It is lighter than air and will rise. You can stay below it if you get down on your hands and knees and crawl as you leave the building.

STEP 3 Find out if there is fire on the other side of a closed door before you open it. Touch it, and the door knob, with the back of your hand. If you feel heat, there is fire, so use another way out.

Don't wait for your home to be ablaze before you start to think about how to evacuate it. Having an escape plan in advance will save you valuable minutes in a fire emergency.

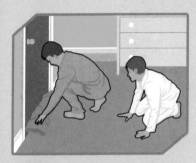

STEP 4 If flames and smoke force you into a fire-free room, close the door behind you and cover the bottom of it with cloth to create a barrier against the smoke and heat outside.

STEP 5 Shout out of the window for help. Tell whoever answers your calls how many people are in the building so they can pass on this information to the fire services.

STEP 6 Don't jump from high windows. The strongest person with you should lower everybody into the arms of an adult on the ground.

ESCAPE PLAN

- Plan two escape routes from each room in the building: the route you normally use and an additional route, which could be a window.

- Choose a meeting place outside the building, where everyone can show up in one place, so that you know who is safe and who needs to be rescued.

- Decide in advance who will assist the very young, elderly or the less able members of your household.

JUMPING SHIP

 STEPS FOR LEAPING OFF

BE PREPARED

- Before you set sail, check that your life raft is seaworthy, so that you can be sure it is fit to be used if there is an emergency.

- Wear your life jacket at all times while you are on the water.

- Make sure your life jacket is the correct size for you and that its zip works properly.

- Only jump off a boat in an emergency and when you have no other option.

- Find out where the lowest decks are so that you know where you could jump from.

STEP 1 If you are not wearing it already, put on your life jacket. Zip it up and fasten the strap securely around your waist so that the jacket doesn't come off.

A fire on your small sailing boat is raging out of control. You can't get to your life raft, so you must jump into the water. But before you take the plunge, there are some safety steps that you should consider.

STEP 2 Move to the lowest part of the vessel. The closer you are to the water, the less chance there is of you injuring yourself when you jump in. Check the water below for debris.

STEP 3 If there is no debris, get ready to leap. Pinch your nose to keep out seawater, grasp your elbow with your free arm and press the other elbow against your body firmly. Now jump!

STEP 4 Keep your head up and your back straight. Just before you hit the water, cross your legs and feet. This will help to prevent you injuring your ankles on impact with the water.

STEP 5 Keep clear of the sinking vessel, which could pull you under the water as it sinks below the surface. Swim away backwards, using your legs, so that you will be able to see and dodge flying debris if the boat explodes.

STEP 6 As you wait to be rescued, keep warm in the water by drawing up your knees and folding your arms.

STICKY
SITUATIONS

You might find that you need to escape from a situation that is awkward, dangerous or difficult emotionally. It may involve people who want to hurt or humiliate you. There are correct ways to handle these tricky dilemmas. You'll find some of them in this chapter, though don't lose any sleep over supernatural scenarios involving zombies, vampires and aliens – these exist only in movies, books or folk tales.

The chances are that if you are being chased by someone, you'd prefer not to get caught. A few clever moves could help you to shake off a pursuer, even if they can run faster than you.

QUICK GETAWAY

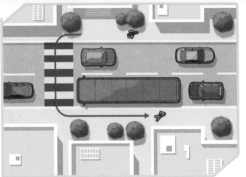

STEP 1 Backtrack as soon as you can do so without being spotted. You could cross a road and run back in the direction you came from, using vehicles to hide you as you go. Your pursuer may not realize you have changed direction and might continue in a straight line.

STEP 2 Blend in with a crowd. Disguise yourself by taking off some clothing items and putting on others.

STEP 3 Hide if you can't run any further. Choose a place where there is another escape route nearby.

A tracker dog only needs one sniff of your clothing to recognize your smell and follow the trail of scent that hangs in the air behind you. Lose a dogged tail and its handler like this.

PUT OFF THE SCENT

STEP 1 Scramble over fences and walls that are too tall for the dog to climb. Then try to stay downwind of the dog so that it can't pick up your scent in the air.

STEP 2 Wade through ponds and rivers whenever you can to break the trail of scent. Move close to greenery along the water's edge, so that you are less easy to spot from a distance.

STEP 3 If the dog persists, jump on a bike and speed off on it. You will cut off the scent trail by doing this, and it is unlikely that the dog or its handler will be able to keep up with you.

If someone sneaks up behind you and locks their arms around yours, you will feel like you are being hugged by a bear. These steps will get you out of this grizzly situation.

SHRUG OFF THE HUG

STEP 1 Practise your bear-hug escape with a friend so that you perform it instinctively, making it less likely that you will panic if it happens to you for real.

STEP 2 Shove your bottom into the attacker while thrusting your arms upwards. This will loosen the attacker's hold and move their arms up to your shoulders.

AVOID ATTACKS

- Stick to well-lit, busy places.
- Don't wander aimlessly looking lost, even if you are lost.
- Pay attention. You are an easy target for attackers when you are distracted by music on your headphones, talking on the phone or reading a map.
- If you think you are being followed, go directly to a shop, café or other place where there are people around.

STEP 3 Grab the attacker's wrists and push them up above your head. Bend your knees as you do this so that you can duck underneath the attacker's arms.

Use these moves if an attacker grabs you by the wrist. Even if they are stronger, you will be able to escape their grip and then throw them off balance to give yourself time to get away.

FLIP OF THE WRIST

STEP 1 If someone grabs your wrist, make a fist with the hand of your gripped arm. Grasp the underside of your fist firmly with your free hand.

STEP 2 Turn your joined hands through 180°. This move will cross the attacker's arms and your wrist will slip out through their fingers.

STEP 3 Push the attacker's nearest shoulder. Most of their weight will be on the hip furthest from you, so this shove will throw them off balance.

STEP 4 These boys are friends who are practising the steps, but if you ever get attacked for real, run away as fast as you can at the first opportunity.

Bullies love to get a reaction. So, if the school bully picks on you, stay calm and hide your emotions and they may just give up. If they persist, take these steps to end your torment.

PLAYGROUND PEST

STEP 1 Write down the details of the bullying incidents. When you decide to tell someone, this record will make it easier for you to prove what has been going on.

STEP 1 If you get nasty messages on your computer, don't reply. Print them out and jot down the sender's Internet Protocol (IP) address – you'll find this in the email 'header'.

STEP 2 Ask an adult to contact the bully's Internet Service Provider to have all messages from their IP address to your computer blocked. Run tracking software to find out who the bully is.

CYBERBULLY

You can avoid playground bullies when you are at home, but cyberbullies can reach you there via your computer. Shut down this distressing behaviour using this advice.

STEP 2 Tell a teacher about the situation. Your school may already have a way of dealing with bullying, in which case the teacher will know what to do to sort out the problem.

STEP 3 Make a joke of it. Your replies to whatever the bully says don't have to be witty, but it helps to have an answer ready. The bully might decide that you are too clever to pick on.

STEP 3 If the bully continues to harass you by using a different computer, visit their home so that you can speak to their guardian about the problem. Show them your evidence of the bullying and ask them to get their child to stop it.

STEP 4 Shake hands and agree that the matter is closed if the bully apologizes to you. If, however, the bully doesn't stop – and particularly if they make threats of violence – contact the police, who will be able to help you with the matter.

NIGHTMARE SCENARIO

STEP 1 Use a night-light. If you wake up from a nightmare, you'll be able to see familiar things around you and this should make you feel more comfortable, allowing you to get back to sleep.

STEP 2 Keep a dream diary. As soon as you wake up in the morning, write down the details of your nightmare, the time you went to bed, what you did just before resting and how you were feeling at the time.

If you have nightmares regularly, there is something in your life that is causing them. These steps will help you to find out what that is and show you how you can turn your nightmares into pleasant dreams.

STEP 3 Show your dream diary to an adult that you trust. By talking things through with another person, you may be able to discover what is causing your nightmares and then you can do something about them.

STEP 4 Do physical activities that you enjoy. They will distract you from things that might be worrying you and giving you the nightmares. The exercise will also tire you out so that you sleep longer without interruptions.

STEP 5 Try to control your dreams. Give them a happy or funny ending. For example: if you dream about monsters under your bed, imagine an adult stomping on their hands and scaring them off.

POSSIBLE CAUSES

- 🔆 Being too tired because you are not in a regular sleeping routine (in which you go to bed and wake up at the same times every day).

- 🔆 Reading scary books or watching spooky films just before bedtime.

- 🔆 A traumatic event, such as a death in your family.

- 🔆 Stress caused by exams, bullies (see pp.94–95) or other things that are making you anxious.

- 🔆 Eating just before you go to bed.

Extra-terrestrials would be just as curious about us as we are about them. If an alien tries to abduct you for its experiments, follow these steps and make it go home without you.

ALIEN EVASION

STEP 1 Resist the alien's mind-control rays by focussing your thoughts on the word 'no'. If you have aluminium foil, make a hat for extra protection against the rays. A saucepan on your head would also work.

STEP 1 Slow down the robot by moving randomly in a zig-zag. Make each zig and zag a different number of steps so that the droid's tracking software can't predict your next move.

AVOID THE DROID

Future human-like robots, or androids, will travel in a straight line faster than you can sprint. So, if they suddenly go berserk, how can you escape their cold death-grip and burning lasers?

STEP 2 An alien's body might not be able to cope with the bacteria and viruses in our breath, so try to contaminate your visitor by coughing, sneezing or breathing heavily on it. This should make it back off.

STEP 3 Shout and bang objects to create lots of noise. The last thing that the alien would want to do is draw attention to its abduction attempt, so it would soon run away and zoom off in its spaceship.

STEP 2 Run from shaded areas into direct sunlight or another source of bright light, such as a street lamp. As the robot tries to track you using its vision sensors, the sudden change in light intensity will confuse it.

STEP 3 Create obstacles for the heavy, bulky robot: clamber over walls or cars, jump over hedges and crawl under bushes. Avoid stairs – the robot's sophisticated software will be programmed to deal with them.

SO LONG, SUCKER!

 VAMOOSE FROM A VAMPIRE

STEP 1 Run into sunlight, which causes vampires to burst into flames. This vampire is lucky that he just got his toe burnt. It would have been a different story if he had ventured fully into the light.

STEP 2 Hold up a cross – this is a Christian symbol. Many vampires were Christians before they became bloodsuckers. The cross reminds them of this time and makes them feel guilty about attacking you.

STEP 3 Surround yourself with garlic and eat some of it. Garlic contains a chemical called allicin. This smells like rotting flesh to vampires, who like their victims to be fresh. Garlic also thins human blood – vampires prefer it to be thicker.

VAMPIRE TRAITS

- Pale skin – they are never in the sunshine so there is no chance of them getting a tan.
- Long, pointy canine teeth, which they sink into the flesh of their victims to extract the blood.
- Their image does not reflect in a mirror.
- They sleep in coffins during the day and get particularly angry if you disturb them while they are sleeping.

Vampires feed on the blood of the living. They usually hunt for their victims at night, so you can avoid them most of the time. In the unlikely event that you bump into a vampire, do the following things to avoid its fangs.

STEP 4 If there is no garlic around, spill rice on the floor. Vampires are fanatical counters, so your pursuer won't be able to resist trying to find out how many grains there are. Sneak away while he is distracted.

STEP 5 Be warned: your vampire could be a particularly fast counter and may catch up with you. If this is the case, get yourself to a river and make your way to the opposite bank. This will really frustrate the vampire, who can't cross running water because it drains his powers.

STEP 6 If there isn't a river nearby, race into a church. There are far too many crosses in the building for the vampire to cope with, and he is sure to give up the chase. Wait until the morning before you come out.

ZOMBIE ATTACK

 RUN FROM THE WALKING DEAD

STEP 1 Pack rucksacks with food, water and bedding. Prepare to be away from your home for several days while the authorities get the zombies under control.

STEP 2 Race to a building on high ground with a good view of the surroundings, where you can watch out for zombies easily. If you meet a zombie on the way, pretend to be one.

STEP 3 Barricade yourselves into the building by boarding up the windows and doors, but make sure you have one escape route, just in case the zombies burst into the building.

Flesh-eating zombies are on the rampage near your home. A single bite or scratch from one would turn you into a walking corpse. They don't feel pain, so don't try to defend yourself against them – evacuate the area.

STEP 4 Take it in turns to keep watch. While one person is on look-out, the others should get some rest. Work in shifts of four hours – you won't be able to concentrate for much longer than this.

STEP 5 If friends come seeking refuge, don't let them in until you are sure they haven't been bitten or scratched by a zombie. Turn your friends away if you see marks.

STEP 6 Listen to the radio, or check the internet, for news reports. The authorities will let you know when they have rounded up the zombies and it is safe to go home.

DEAD GIVEAWAYS

- The zombie walk – their undead bodies are stiff so they walk without bending their knees and hold out their arms in front.
- A brain-dead stare that makes them look dazed.
- A moaning sound – like the one you make when you have a pain in your stomach.
- A foul smell, which comes from their rotting flesh.

ESCAPE ESSENTIALS

BE PREPARED

TIP 1 Always take a survival kit with you on a trip to the great outdoors. These items are 'must-haves' – you may need to add other things to your kit, depending on the climate and conditions.

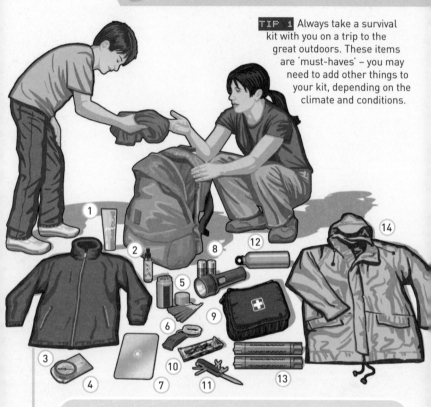

SURVIVAL KIT 'MUST-HAVES'

1. Sunscreen
2. Mosquito spray
3. Fleece top
4. Compass
5. Matches in a waterproof holder
6. Emergency whistle
7. Heliograph
8. Torch and spare batteries
9. First-aid kit
10. High-energy bar
11. Multi-purpose tool
12. Water in a water bottle
13. Emergency flares
14. Waterproof jacket

Whether you are stranded in the wild, dealing with a dangerous animal or caught up in an accident or emergency, being prepared ahead of the situation will increase your chances of escaping it.

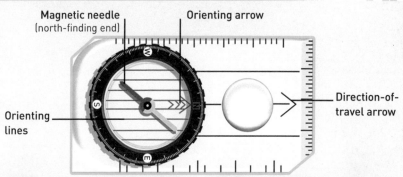

Magnetic needle (north-finding end)

Orienting arrow

Orienting lines

Direction-of-travel arrow

TIP 2 To find your bearings: 1) Hold your compass flat – the north-finding end of the needle will point north. 2) Turn the dial until the orienting arrow and red end of the needle are lined up. Now you know which way south, east and west are, too.

TIP 3 To fix a direction on your compass: 1) Aim the direction-of-travel arrow at your target. 2) Turn the dial to line up the red end of the needle and the orienting arrow. 3) Keep them lined up as you travel and you will stay on course.

TIP 4 You need a good level of physical fitness to perform most of the escapes in this book. For a healthy heart and lungs, do exercises that get you out of breath. Build up strength in your muscles by doing resistance exercises, such as press-ups.

TIP 5 Plan for accidents and emergencies. For example: get together with your family and draw a floor plan with fire escape routes from your home. This will show you the best way out at-a-glance. Practise your fire drill regularly.

TIP 6 Make sure you can use the correct signals in an emergency by practising them with your friends.

DISTRESS SIGNALS

SIGNAL 1 If you run into a problem underwater while diving (see pp.18–19), you'll need assistance as soon as you surface. Signal your distress to the dive-boat crew by extending out one arm to your side and waving it up and down.

SIGNAL 2 Be sure to use the correct flare if you need to signal for help from a life raft. Daytime flares are held in the hand and produce orange smoke. Shoot night-time flares up into the sky to create a firework effect.

SIGNAL 3 Three short whistle blasts every minute is a distress signal in most mountain areas of the world. But, if you are in the United Kingdom or the European Alps, blow your whistle six times instead.

Signalling for help could be your only means of escape from a survival situation. But what type of signal should you use? This depends on where you are, the time of day and the location of the person you are signalling to.

SIGNAL 4 To signal for help using a heliograph, first direct sunlight onto the ground using the mirrored side of the device. Then, look through the hole in the heliograph to guide the light upwards onto an aircraft or ship.

SIGNAL 5 Inform the pilot of an aircraft that you need to be picked up by forming a Y-shape with your body and arms.

SIGNAL 6 Signal to aircraft or ships for help by building three fires, either in a triangle or a line. Make sure that any fire you burn doesn't get out of control and spread.

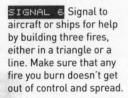

SIGNAL 7 Spell out the letters SOS by scraping their shapes in sand or forming them with objects. The letters are a well-known signal for 'help'.

ALIEN
A foreign being from another planet.

ANDROID
A robot that looks a bit like a human.

ARCTIC
The region around the North Pole.

AVALANCHE
A mass of snow and ice that tumbles down a mountainside rapidly.

BAIT
Food used to attract prey, such as fish or other animals.

BARRICADE
To block an entrance with a makeshift barrier.

CANINE TEETH
Pointy teeth or fangs in the top jaw. They are also known as 'eye teeth'.

CARBON DIOXIDE
A colourless gas made up of oxygen and carbon.

CHRISTIAN
A person who was baptized into a Christian religion, or who is a follower of the teachings of Jesus Christ.

COMPASS
An instrument with a magnetized pointer that shows the direction of north and bearings from it.

CREVASSE
A deep crack in a glacier.

CYBERBULLY
A person who uses communication technology to harass, threaten or embarrass another person.

DEBRIS
Scattered fragments of something that was wrecked or destroyed.

DECIBEL (dB)
A unit used to measure the loudness of sound.

DEHYDRATED
You are dehydrated if you have lost a large amount of water from your body.

DISMOUNT
To get off something that you are riding, such as a horse or bicycle.

EXTRA-TERRESTRIAL *see* ALIEN

FALLOUT
Radioactive particles that are carried into the air after a nuclear accident or explosion.

FROSTBITE
Injury to tissues in the body. It is caused by extremely cold temperatures.

HANDLER
A person who deals with or looks after a certain type of animal.

HELIOGRAPH
A mirrored signalling device that reflects sunlight.

HYPERBARIC CHAMBER
A sealed chamber in which the air pressure can be controlled.

INTERNATIONAL SPACE STATION
A large habitable satellite that orbits the Earth.

INTERNET PROTOCOL ADDRESS
The address of a computer on the internet.

JUNCTION
A place where two or more paths or roads join together.

LIFE JACKET
A sleeveless jacket that keeps a person afloat in water.

MAZE
An arrangement of hedges and paths designed as a 3-dimensional puzzle.

ORIENT
To work out your position with reference to another point, such as north.

OXYGEN
A colourless gas that makes up about 21 per cent of the air that we breathe.

PERSONAL FLOATATION DEVICE
see **LIFE JACKET**

PRESSURE
The continuous physical force applied to the surface of an object by something in contact with it.

PRISONER OF WAR
A person who has been captured and imprisoned by the enemy during a war.

RADIOACTIVE
Something that is giving off heat energy created by the decay of unstable atoms.

REPELLENT
A substance that keeps away particular insects or other pests.

RESPIRATOR
Something that is worn over the mouth and nose to stop a person from inhaling dust, smoke or gases.

SUFFOCATING
Smothering, or causing difficulty in breathing.

VAMPIRE
A fictional creature that rises from its grave at night to drink the blood of the living by biting their necks.

VENOM
A liquid poison produced by some animals.

ZOMBIE
A person whose dead body has been brought back to life by a supernatural force, such as witchcraft.

INDEX

rivers 33, 36, 37, 38, 65, 101
rocks 15, 25, 38, 39, 40, 42, 57, 60
  as signals 29, 40, 45, 49
Romero, Sofia 82
ropes 53, 59
rowing 21, 24, 25, 63
rubber 29
running 31, 34, 35, 39, 62, 68, 90

S

sand 30, 31, 42
sea 16–17, 20–21, 24–25, 64, 65
seat belts 8, 11, 14
self-defence 92–93
shade 40, 43
sharks 66
shelters 12, 13, 29, 35, 40, 42, 52,
  61, 68
ships 20–21, 22–23, 25, 29, 86–87
shouting 38, 45, 53, 66, 85
signalling 13, 25, 29, 40, 45, 52, 56,
  105, 106–107
skiing 56
smoke 11, 29, 33, 84, 85
snakes 32, 37
snow 52, 54, 57
SOS 52, 107
South America 36–37
Southern Cross 41
space 10–11
spaceships 10–11, 99
stars 24, 41
storms 24, 32, 42, 68–69, 70–71
straightjackets 82–83
submarines 16–17
sunglasses 43

sunlight 29, 40, 42, 43, 100, 107
sunscreen 43, 104
survival kits 7, 12, 13, 20, 21, 45, 104
sweat 34, 43
swimming 15, 17, 38, 58, 64, 65, 66,
  67, 87

T

tents 34, 35
tornadoes 68–69
tracker dogs 79 91
tracks 33
trails, marking 33, 45, 49, 77
trees 39, 57, 63, 70, 71, 72
tsunamis 62–63, 64
tunnelling 78–79

U

vampires 100–101, 109
volcanoes 60–61

W

warmth 17, 21, 52, 53, 54, 55, 59, 87
water 9, 14–15, 16–17, 18–19, 23, 24,
  30, 35, 36, 38, 58, 62–63, 64–65,
  66–67, 72, 86, 87, 101, 104
  drinking 13, 24, 28, 41, 43, 48, 49, 52
waves 25, 62–63
waving 25, 45, 46, 64
whirlpools 65
whistles 106
wind 34, 42, 54, 60, 68–69, 72
windows 10, 12, 14, 85

Z

zombies 102–103, 109